THE GREAT RACE MAZE

ANNA NILSEN

For Auntie Anne
— From ATB

GET READY TO RACE AROUND THE WORLD!

The race begins at the green flag ⚑ on the left-hand page, which marks the starting point. Navigate your way through the mind-bending maze as fast as you can to reach the red flag ⚑ on the right. Then turn the page and find the next green flag to start the second exciting lap of the race…

ON YOUR MARKS

Beware – danger, detours and hazards await you! (Don't worry if you get lost along the way – the solutions are at the back of the book.) If you survive to the end, then test your skill with the 12 extra puzzles that follow the last maze.

GET SET

Time yourself over each section of the race, and see how long it takes you to complete the whole hair-raising journey. Keep a note of your times and try to improve on your record. You can play against a friend and see who wins. Good luck!

NOW GO!

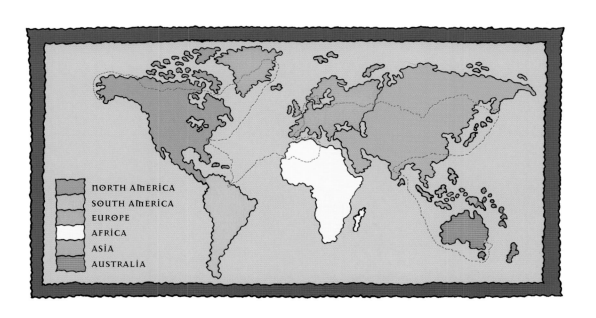

NORTH AMERICA
SOUTH AMERICA
EUROPE
AFRICA
ASIA
AUSTRALIA

THE ARCTIC

Sail through icy seas, race along
pipes and logs – you might
even have to travel by dogsled
to reach the waiting jet.

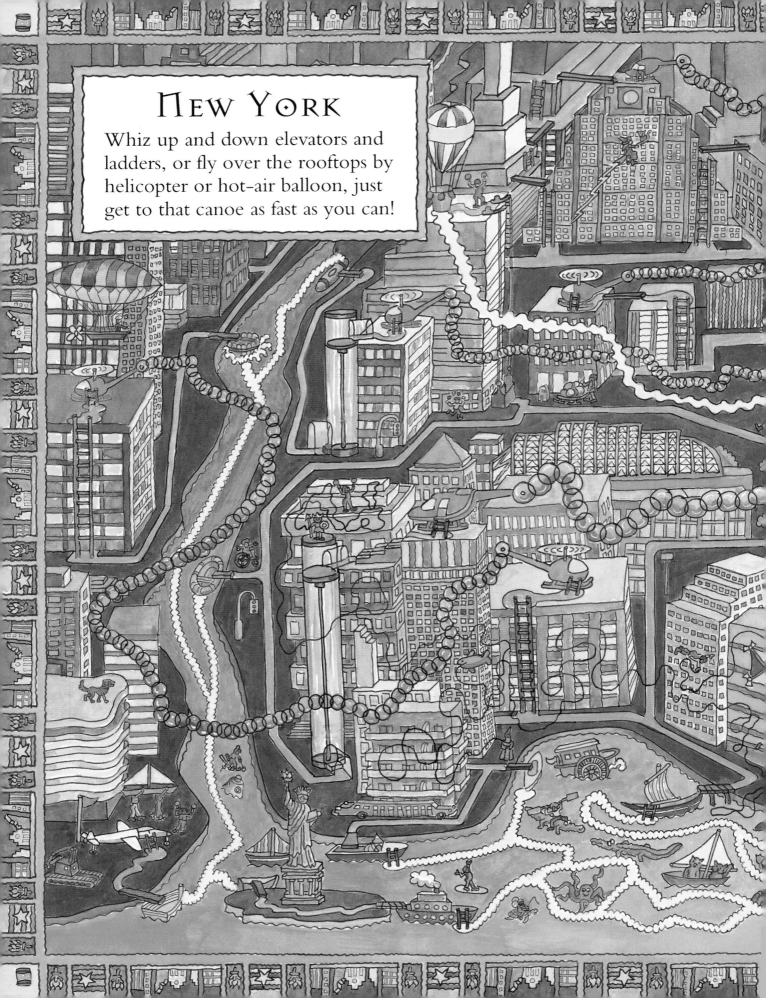

NEW YORK

Whiz up and down elevators and ladders, or fly over the rooftops by helicopter or hot-air balloon, just get to that canoe as fast as you can!

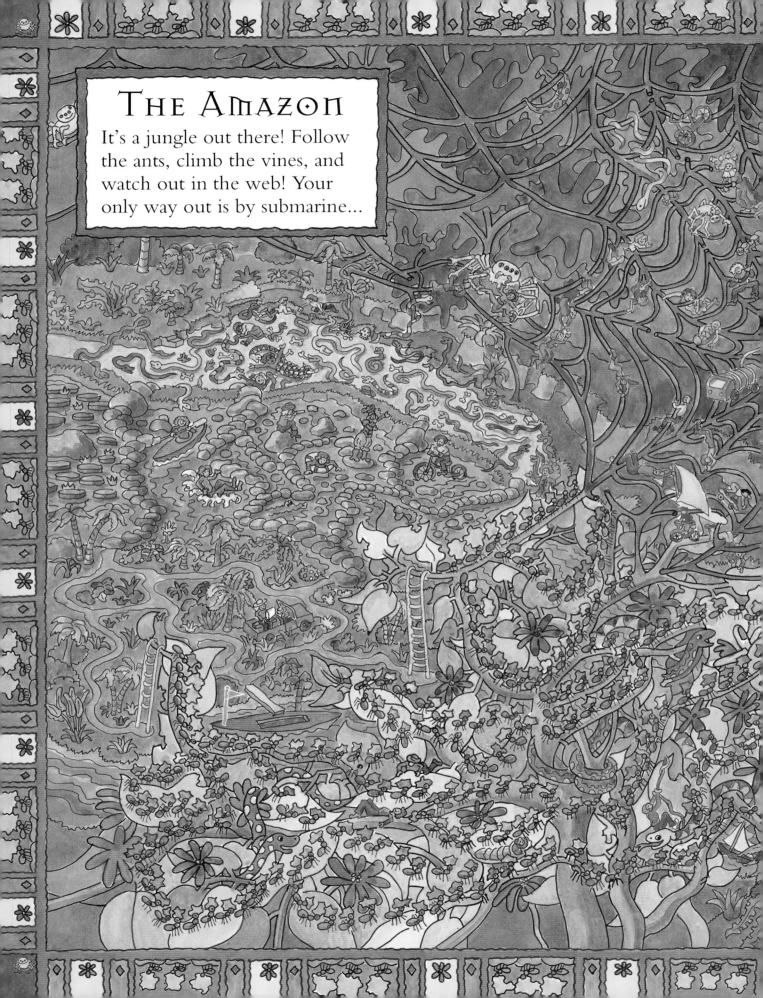

THE AMAZON

It's a jungle out there! Follow the ants, climb the vines, and watch out in the web! Your only way out is by submarine...

THE ATLANTIC

You're really in deep water now!
But if you can follow the tangled
rope to the surface, there's a raft
waiting to give you a lift.

NORTH AFRICA

Travel by sea, track footprints
through the desert or canoe
along rivers – then lift off in
a hot-air balloon!

EUROPE

Brave the wild seas, or ride the lightning bolts. Race across storm-tossed Europe to your magnificent flying machine!

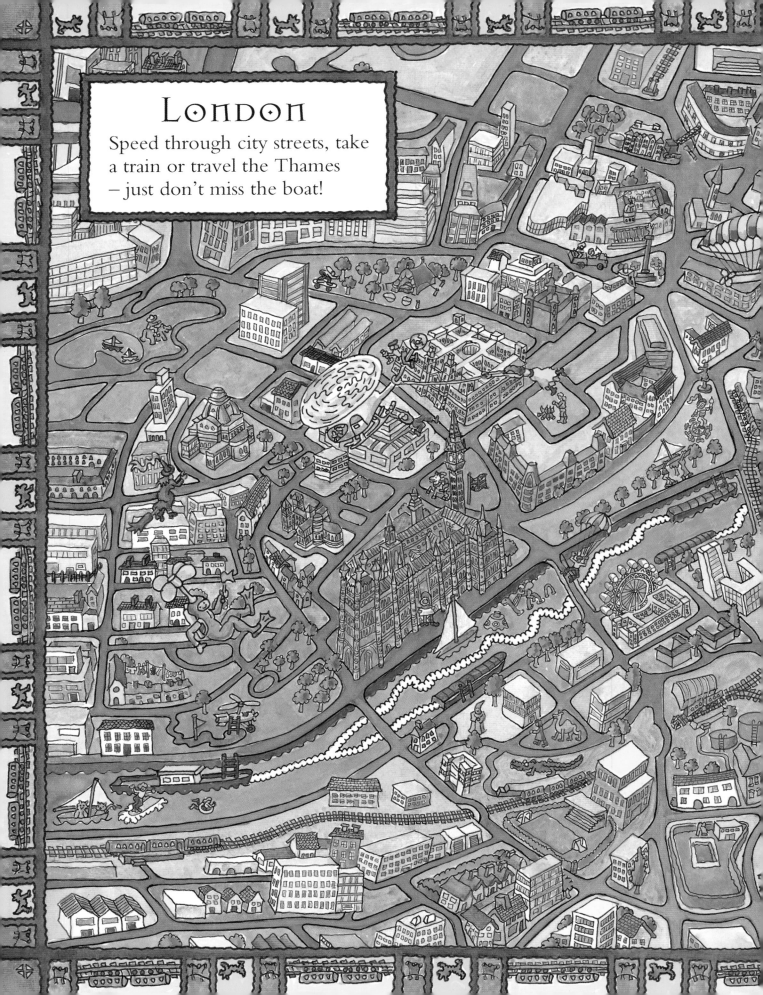

London

Speed through city streets, take
a train or travel the Thames
– just don't miss the boat!

SCANDINAVIA

Go by land, sea or cable car – you have a sleigh ride waiting at the other end.

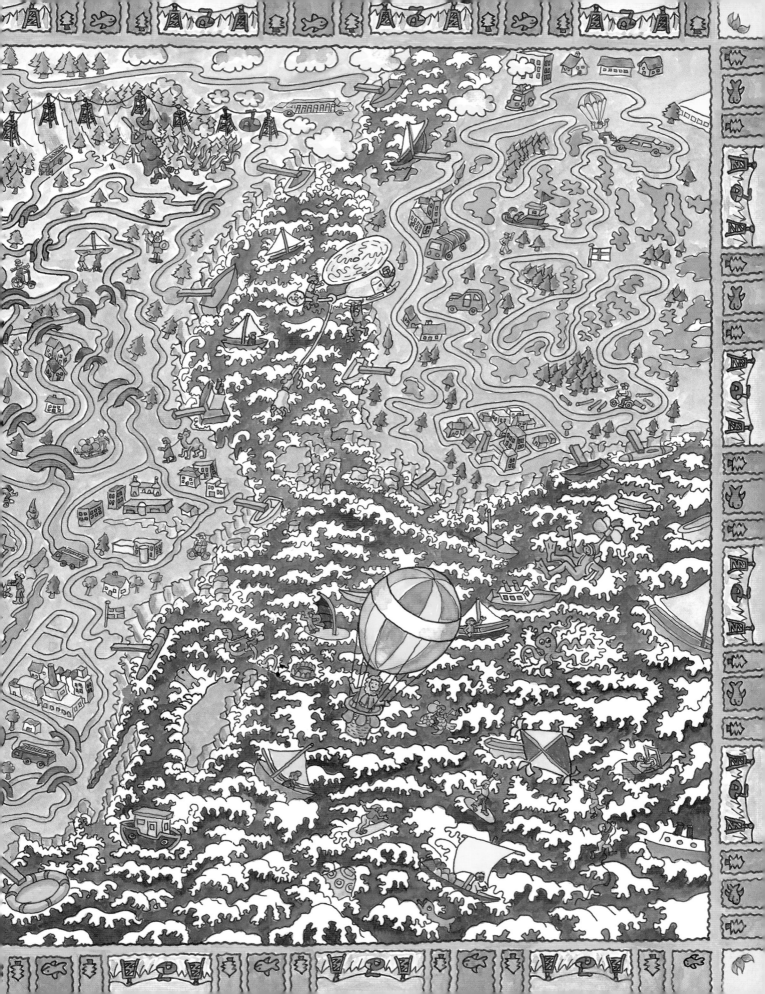

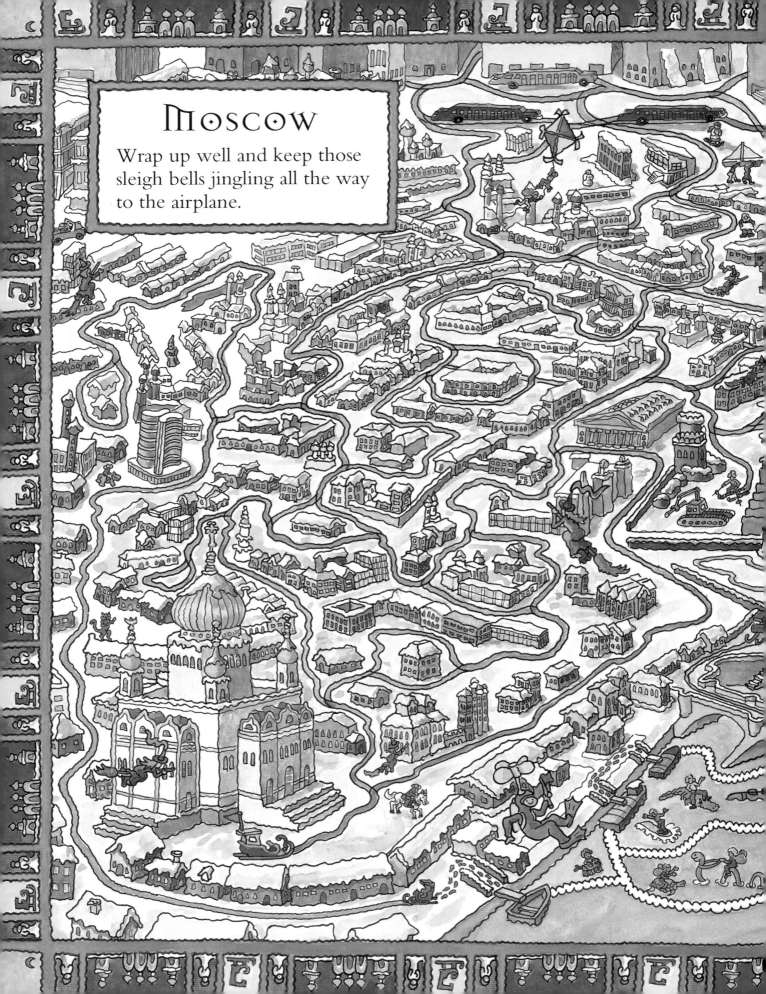

Moscow

Wrap up well and keep those sleigh bells jingling all the way to the airplane.

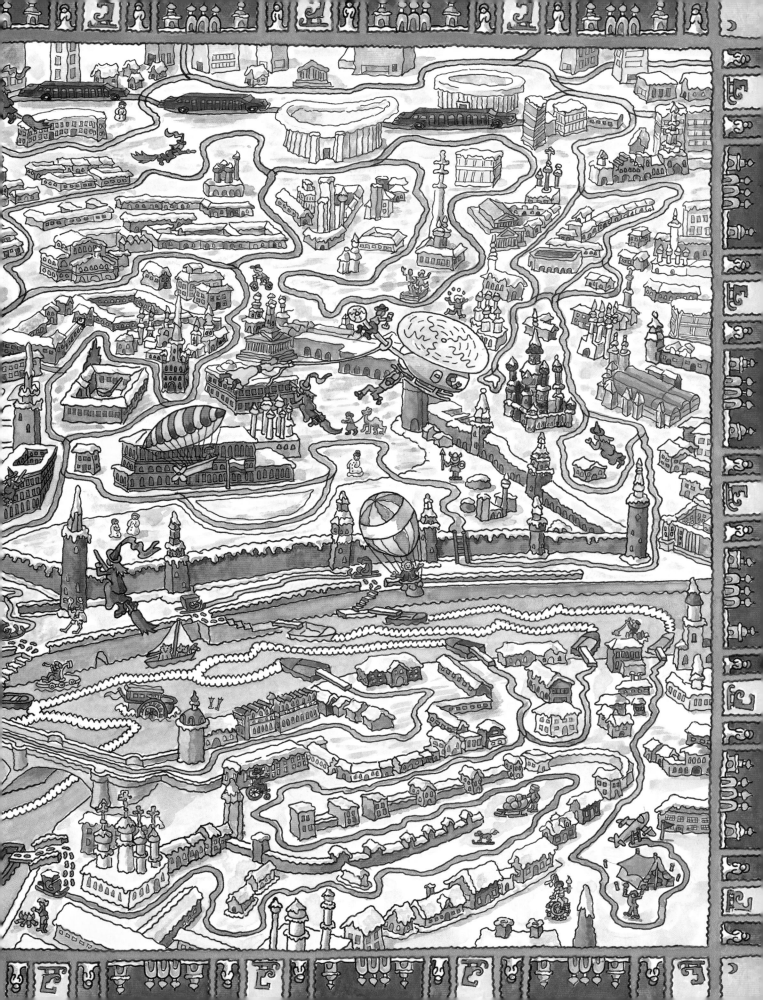

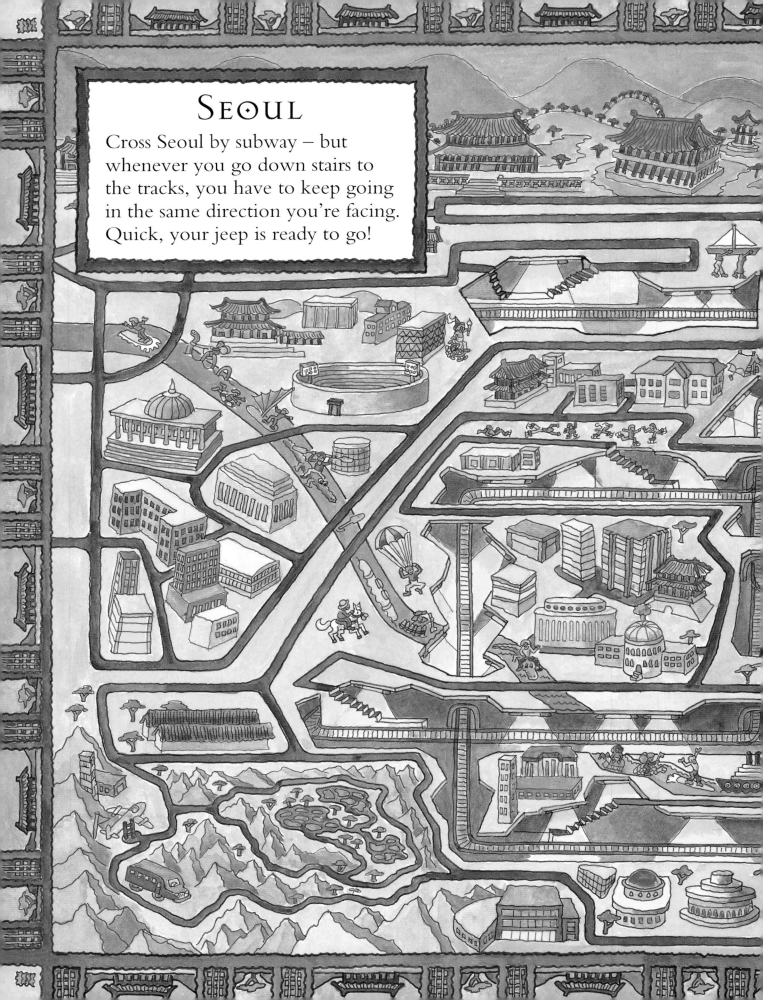

SEOUL

Cross Seoul by subway – but whenever you go down stairs to the tracks, you have to keep going in the same direction you're facing. Quick, your jeep is ready to go!

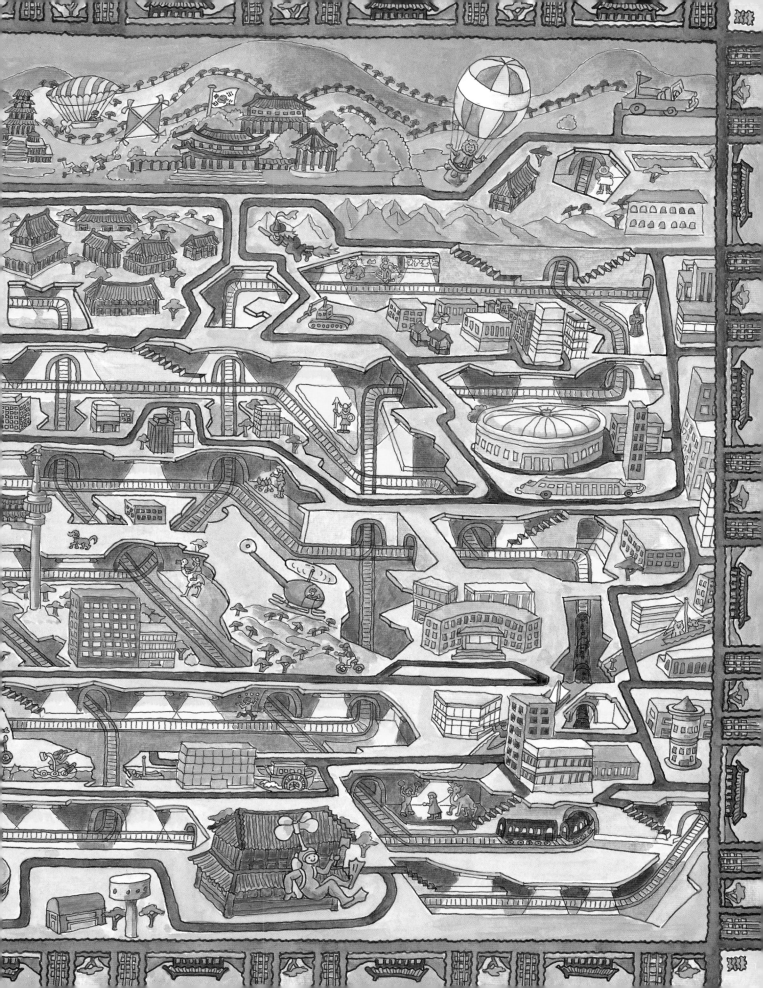

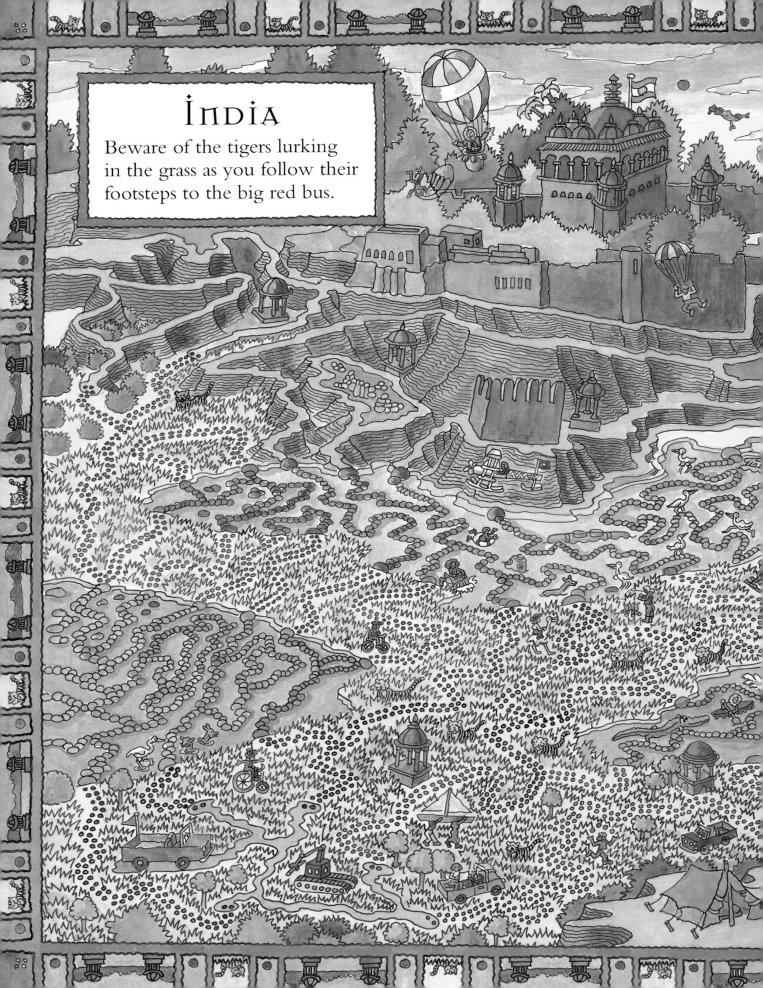

ÎNDÎA

Beware of the tigers lurking in the grass as you follow their footsteps to the big red bus.

SYDNEY

Buzz across the busy harbor to the final flag on the steps of the famous opera house. And the race is won!

PUZZLES

Now you have completed the mazes, let's see if you can go the extra mile and solve these puzzles.

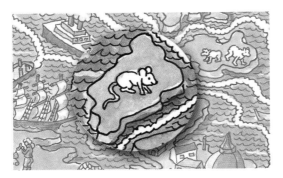

THE ARCTIC
Some of the spectators have been building snow animals. How many can you find? (Don't count the polar bears!)

NEW YORK
Follow the tangled strings to find out who is holding the fish kite.

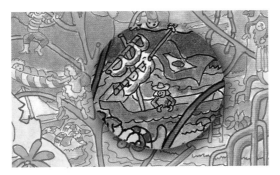

THE AMAZON
Who has stolen the pirate's paddle?

THE ATLANTIC
The diver has lost one of his flippers. Can you find it?

NORTH AFRICA
How many sandy snakes can you find in the desert?

EUROPE
Who set up the ambush that blocked the road? (Hint: Only one character could reach the ambush.)

LONDON

How many topiary animals can you find carved in the bushes?

SCANDINAVIA

The forest is on fire. Can you find a fire engine that can reach the fire and put it out?

MOSCOW

One of the witches has lost her broomstick. Find her broomstick and her black cat.

SEOUL

Help the hippo rider reach the cameleer.

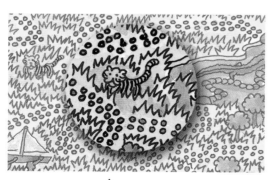

INDIA

How many tigers can you find hidden in the grass?

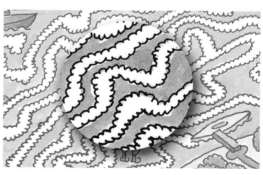

SYDNEY

Can you find a frothy snake hidden in the waves?

Solutions!

These are the most direct routes through the mazes.

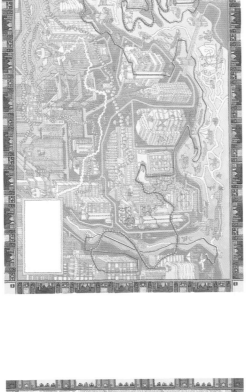

New York

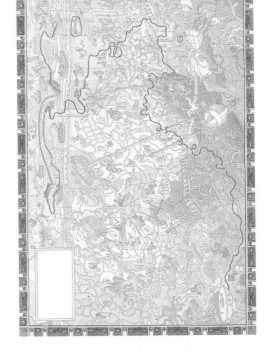

The Atlantic

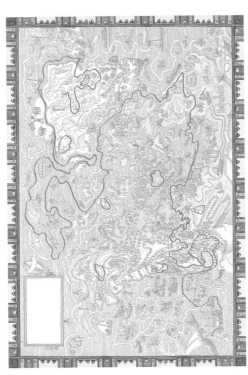

The Arctic

The Amazon

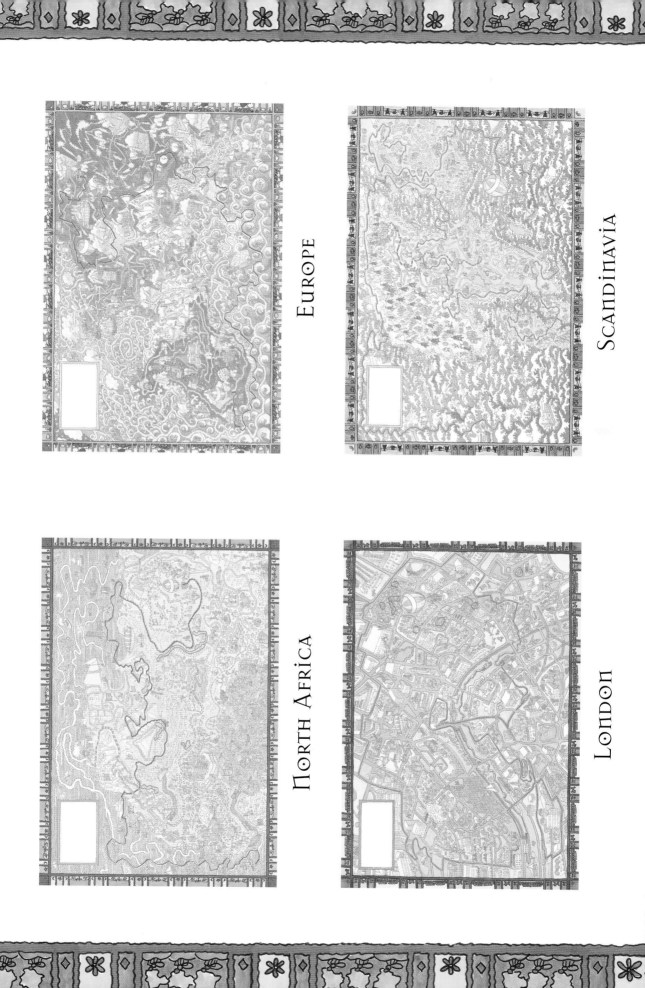

EUROPE

SCANDINAVIA

NORTH AFRICA

LONDON

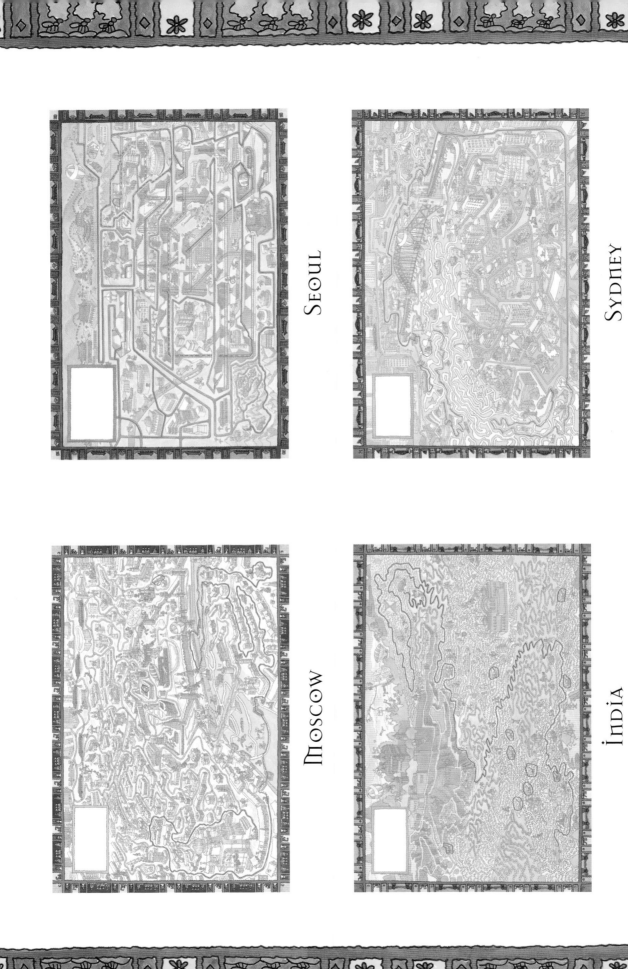

SEOUL

SYDNEY

MOSCOW

INDIA

The aMAZEing journey of... MARCO POLO

ANNA NILSEN

To Fi
- From ATB

Take the journey of a lifetime!

Follow in the footsteps of the explorer Marco Polo in this amazing real-life maze adventure. In 1271, when Marco was only 17, he travelled with his father and uncle from their home in Venice, Italy to the palace of the great emperor Kublai Khan in Khanabalik (now called Beijing), China.

Beware—this is a perilous voyage. You must sail through seas filled with terrifying monsters, climb the world's highest mountains and cross the treacherous Takla Makan Desert.

Start each maze at the green flag on the left-hand page and find your way to the red flag on the right. Then, when you have completed the mazes, there are 12 extra tasks at the back of the book.

Good luck—and safe journey!

The journey of Marco Polo

 Venice

 Roof of the World

 Kanchow

 The Mediterranean

 Kashmir

 Ningxia

 Jerusalem

 Takla Makan Desert

 Shangtu

 Ezerum

 Dunhuang Caves

 Khanabalik

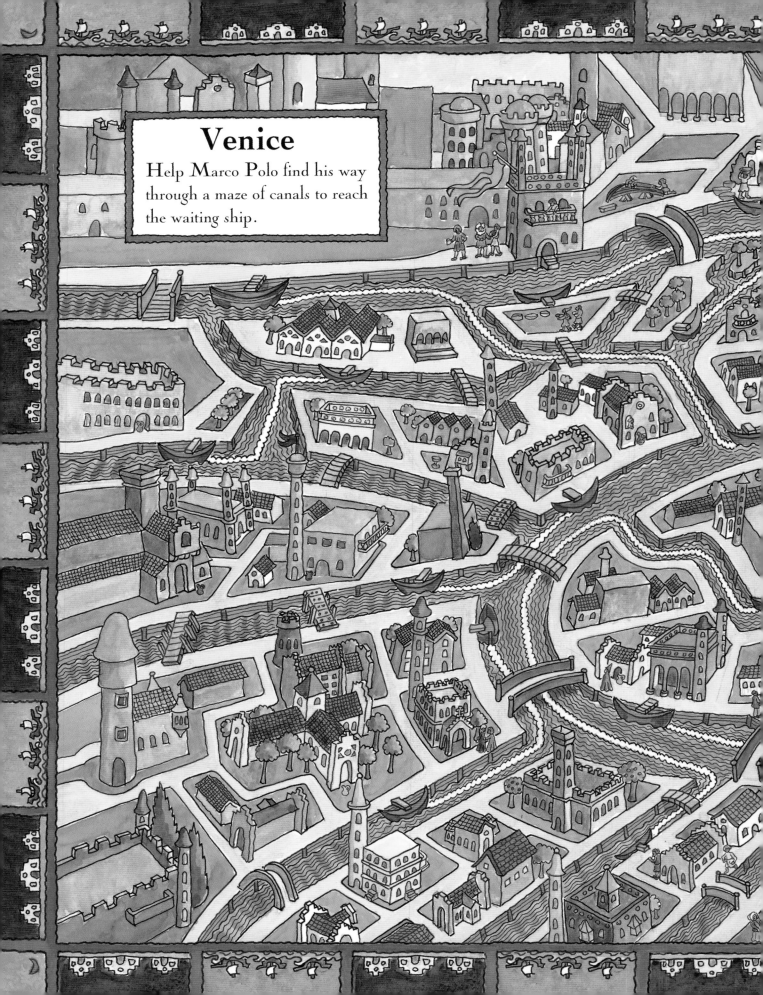

Venice

Help Marco Polo find his way through a maze of canals to reach the waiting ship.

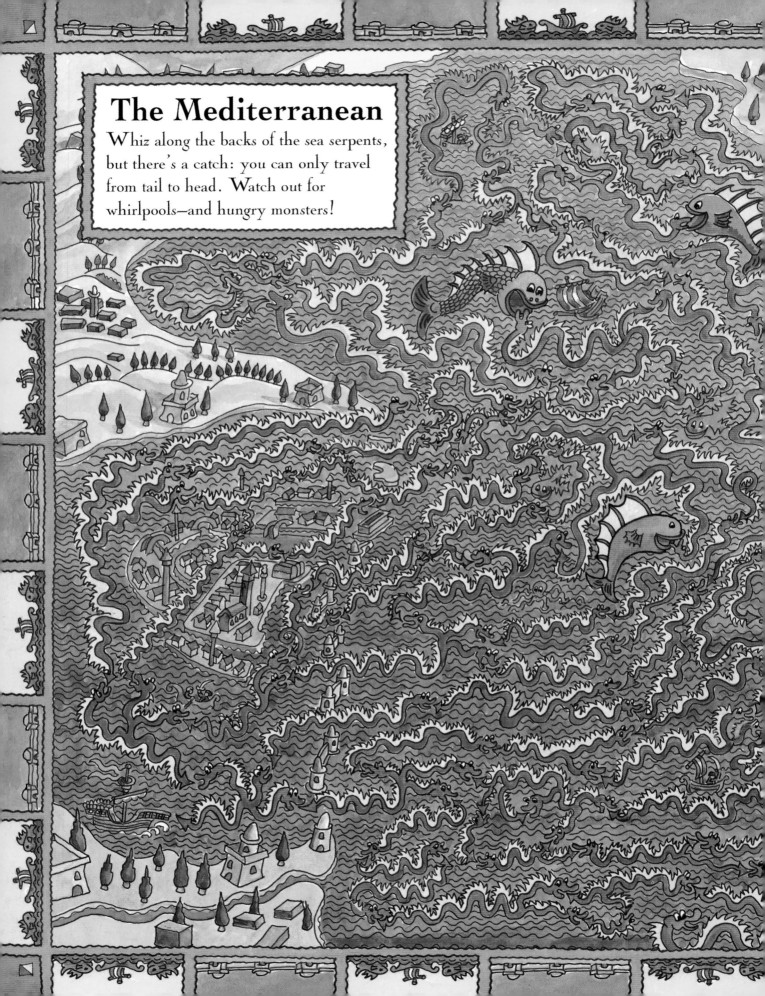

The Mediterranean

Whiz along the backs of the sea serpents, but there's a catch: you can only travel from tail to head. Watch out for whirlpools—and hungry monsters!

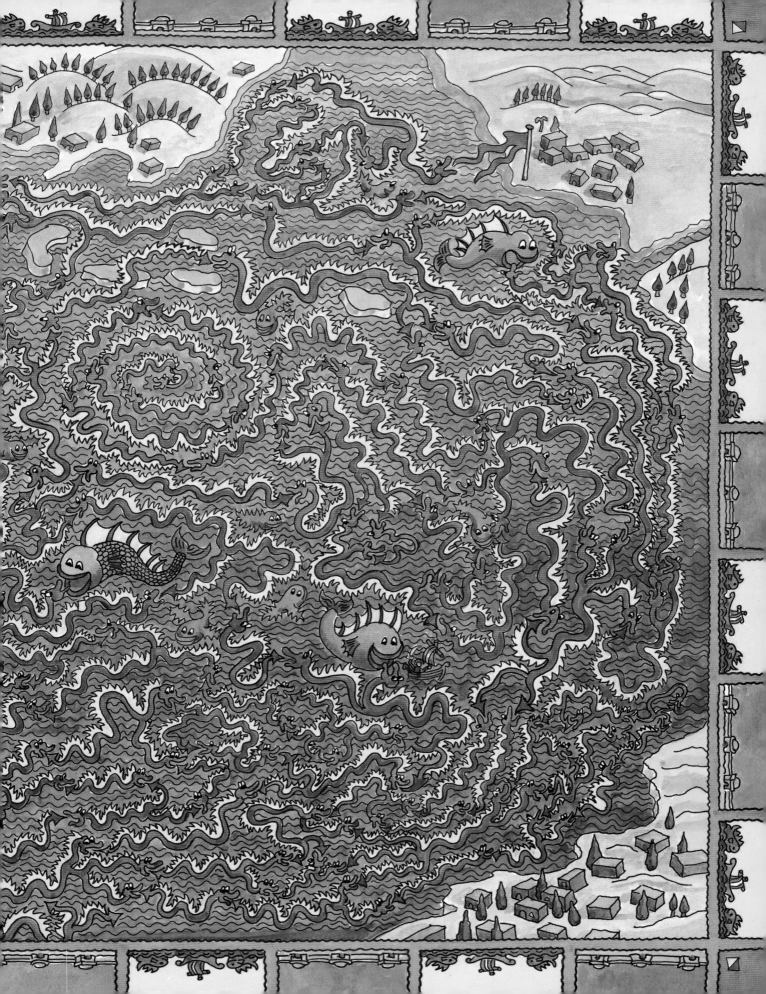

Jerusalem

Take care—you could easily get lost in the winding streets of this holy city!

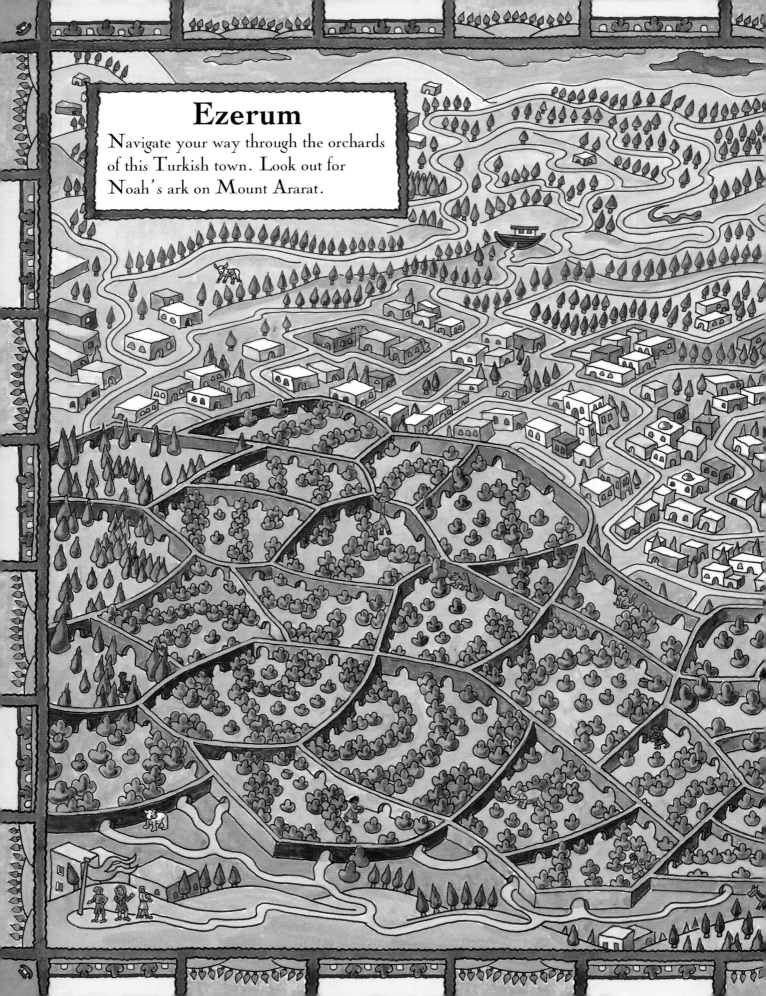

Ezerum

Navigate your way through the orchards of this Turkish town. Look out for Noah's ark on Mount Ararat.

Roof of the World

Pass through the arches and wind your way up and down this rough mountain pass. Take deep breaths—the air is very thin up here!

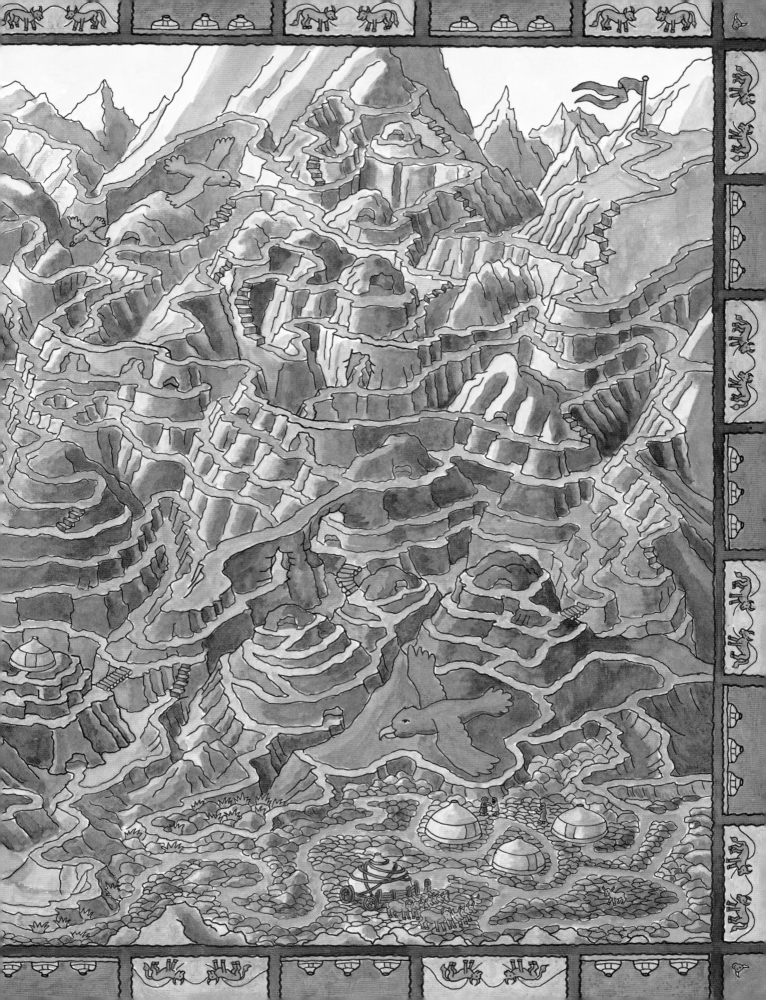

Kashmir

Glide across beautiful lakes and slide down snowy slopes on your way to the highest peak.

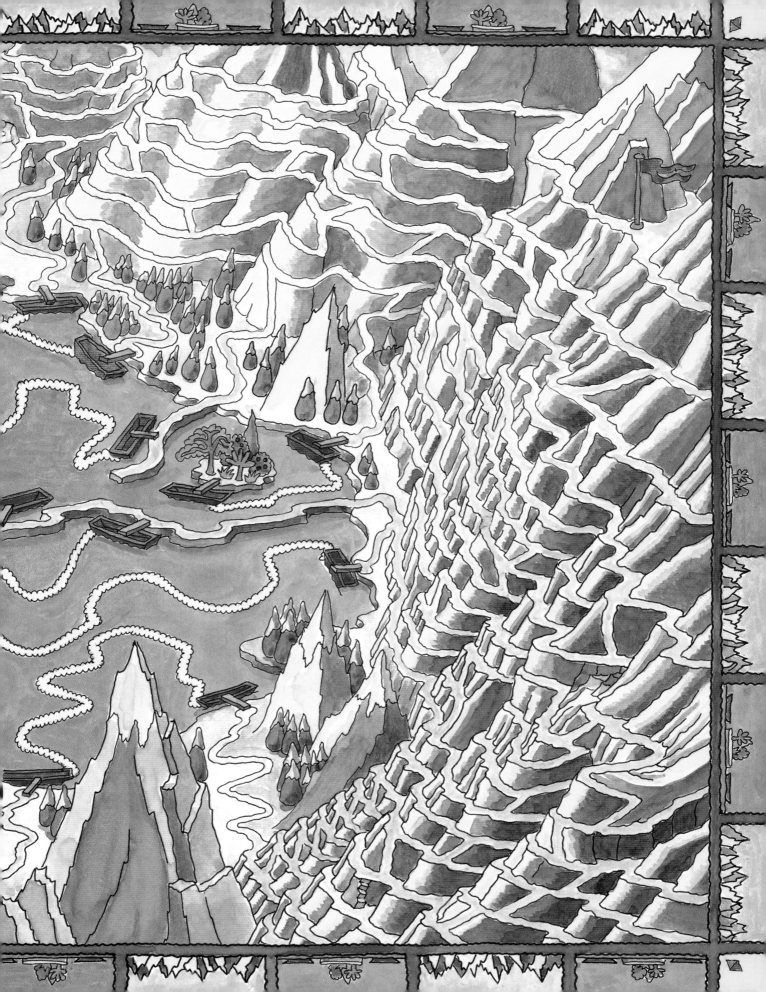

Takla Makan Desert

Trace your path slowly and carefully through the singing sands—many travellers haven't survived...

Dunhuang Caves

Follow the lanterns through the dead of night. Once past the caves, you must climb the craggy cliffs.

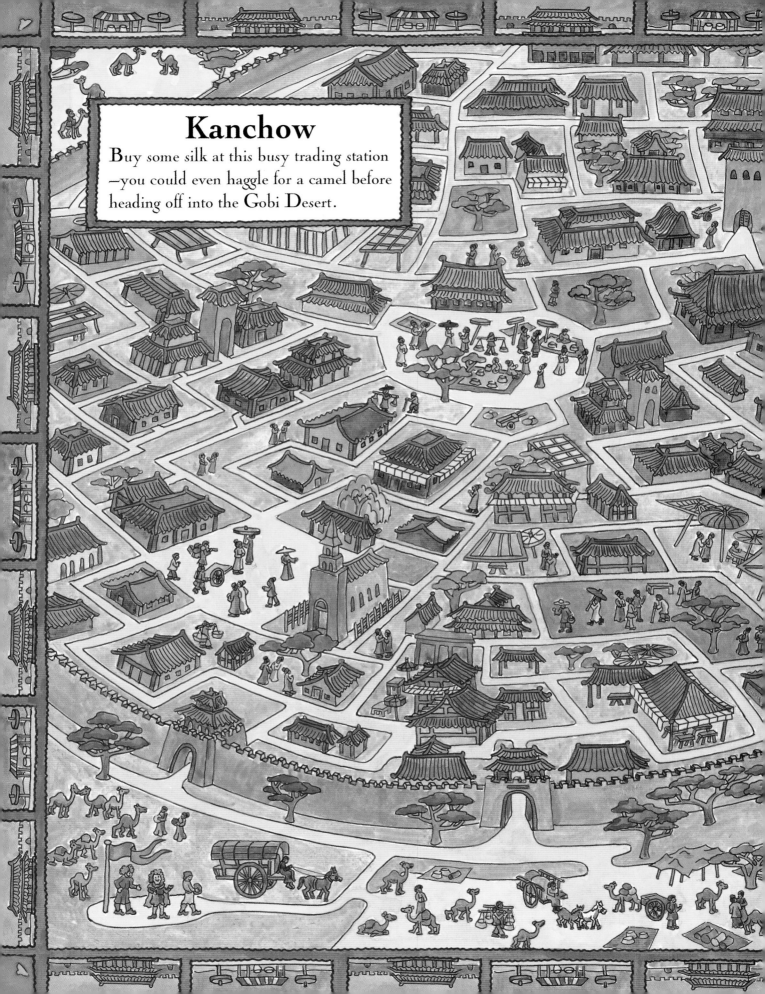

Kanchow

Buy some silk at this busy trading station —you could even haggle for a camel before heading off into the Gobi Desert.

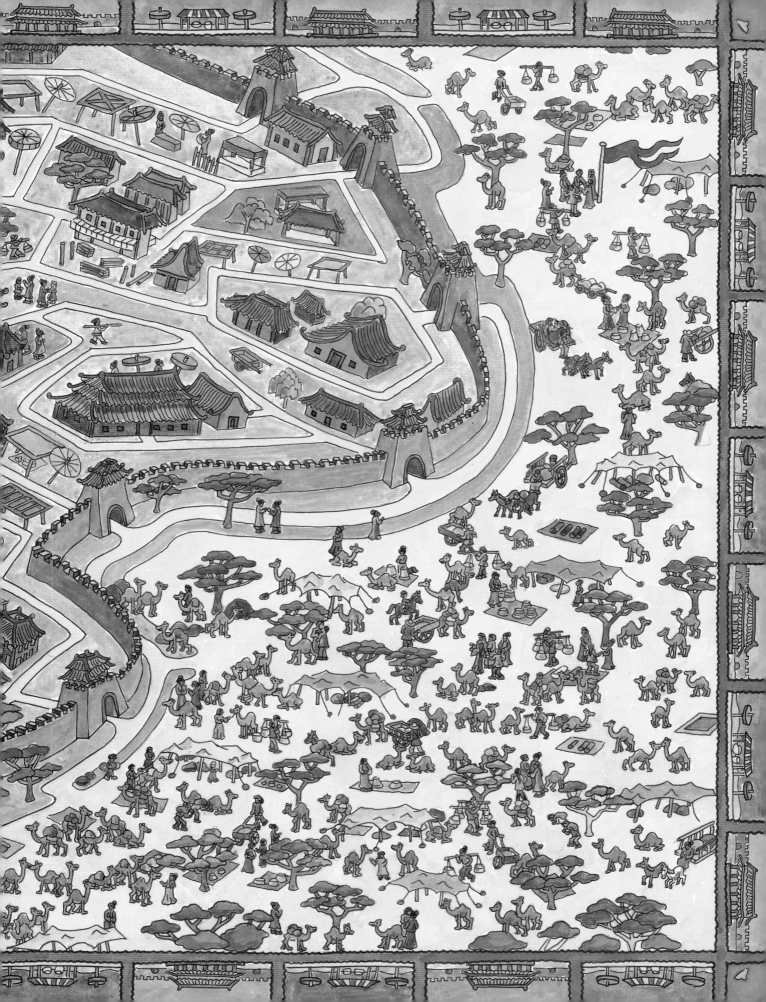

Ningxia

The beautiful bridges, lakes and pagodas of these Chinese gardens are very restful—except if you can't find your way out again!

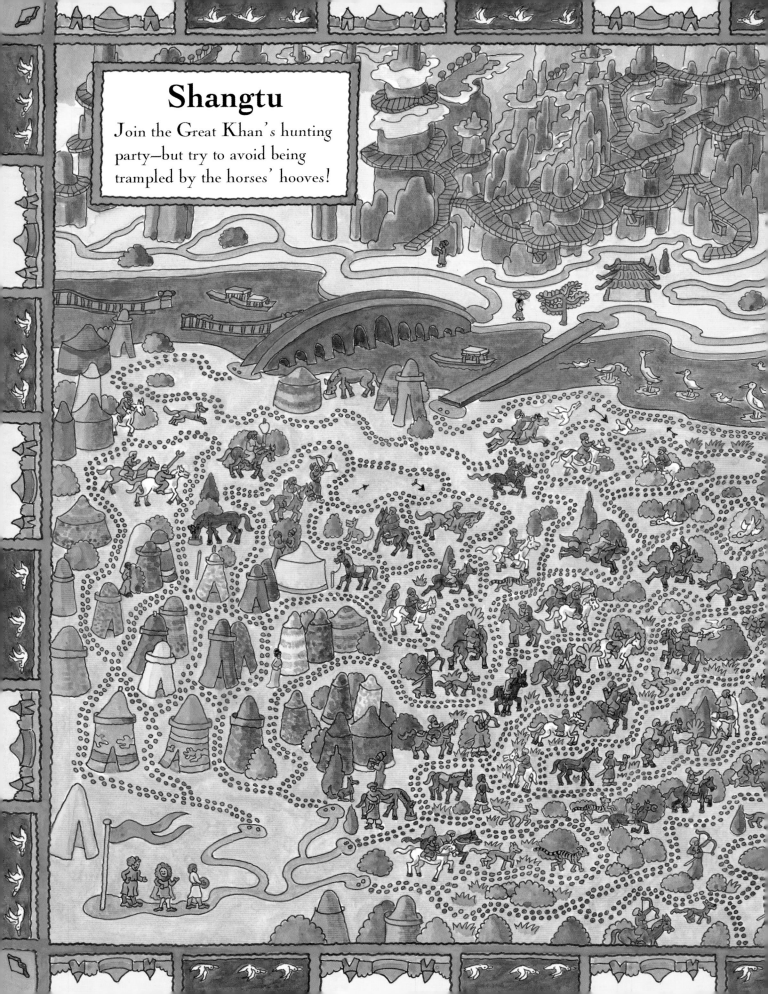

Shangtu

Join the Great Khan's hunting party—but try to avoid being trampled by the horses' hooves!

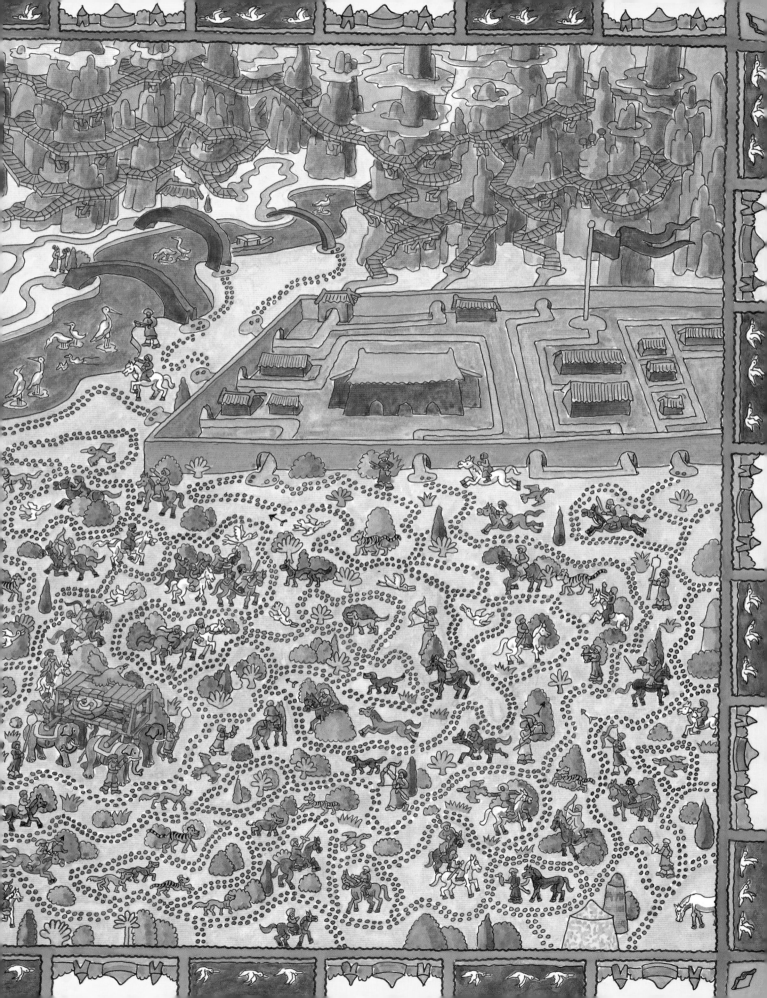

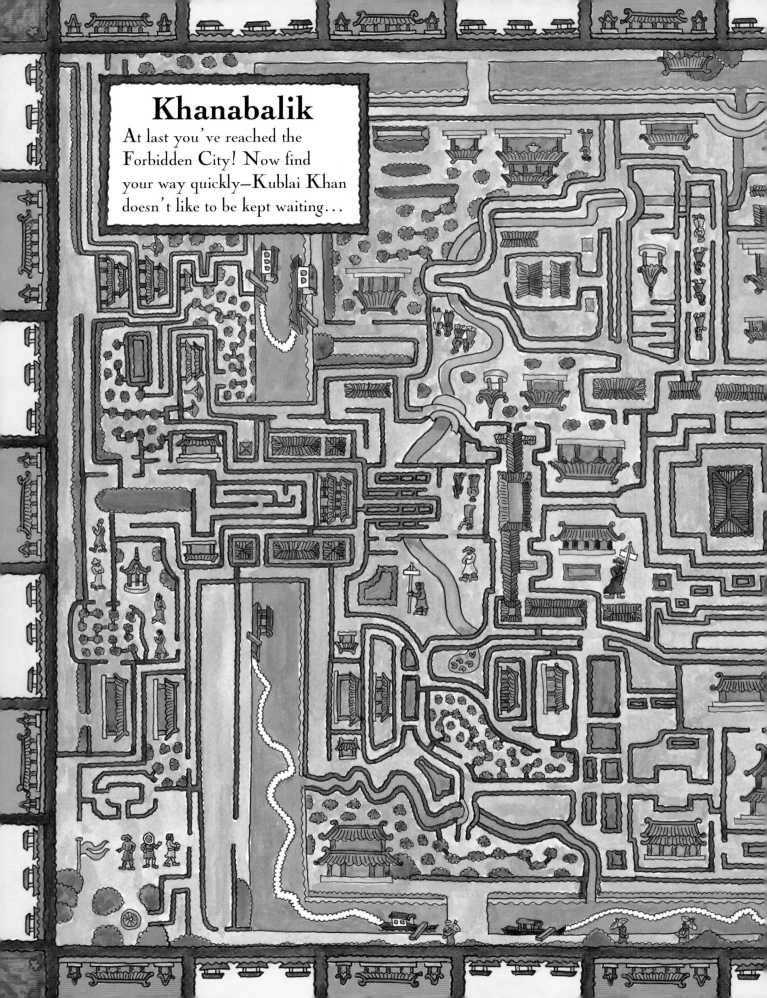

Khanabalik

At last you've reached the
Forbidden City! Now find
your way quickly—Kublai Khan
doesn't like to be kept waiting…

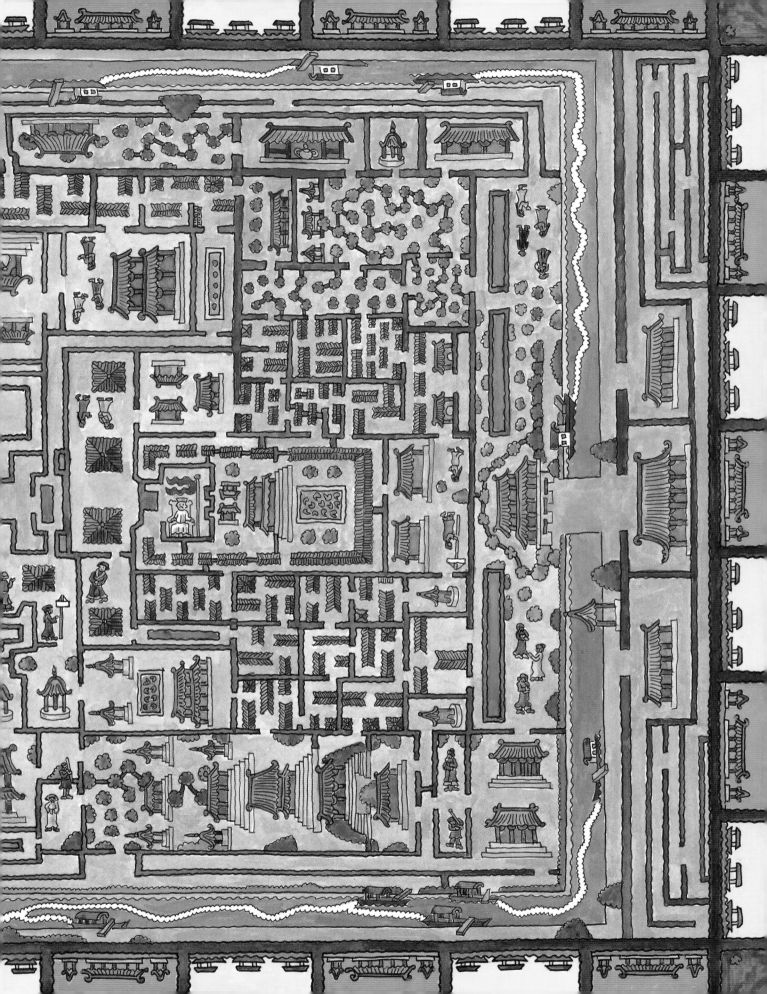

Puzzles
For an extra challenge, try to solve these puzzles.

Venice
How many gold water jugs can you find?

The Mediterranean
How many pirates with gold sabres are
waiting to pounce?

Jerusalem
Help Marco collect the pot of oil from Herod's
temple to take to Kublai Khan.

Ezerum
How many pairs of animals can you find?

Roof of the World
Help Marco reach the yurt being drawn
by cattle.

Kashmir
Can you find the way to the floating garden
in the lake?

Takla Makan Desert
Find the ghostly camel.

Dunhuang Caves
How many priests carrying candles can you find?

Kanchow
Look for a camel with two humps.

Ningxia
How many dragon statues with wings can you find?
Now find one without wings!

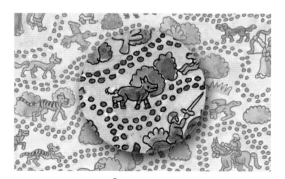

Shangtu
Can you find the wild boar?

Khanabalik
Find the oil, and help Marco deliver
it to Kublai Khan.

Solutions!

These are the most direct routes through the mazes.

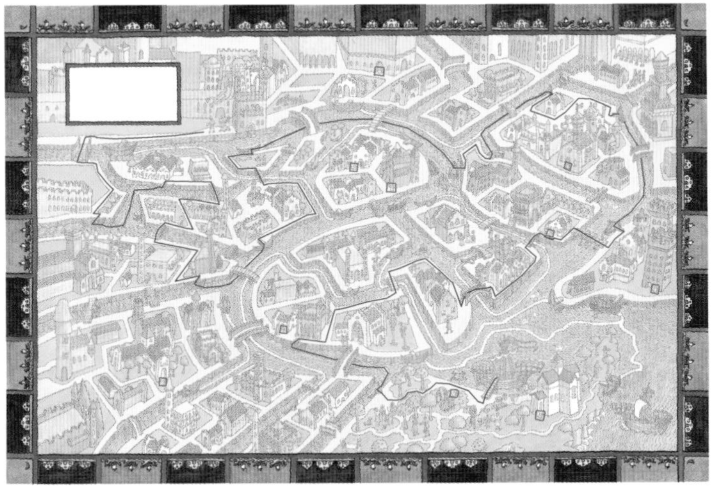

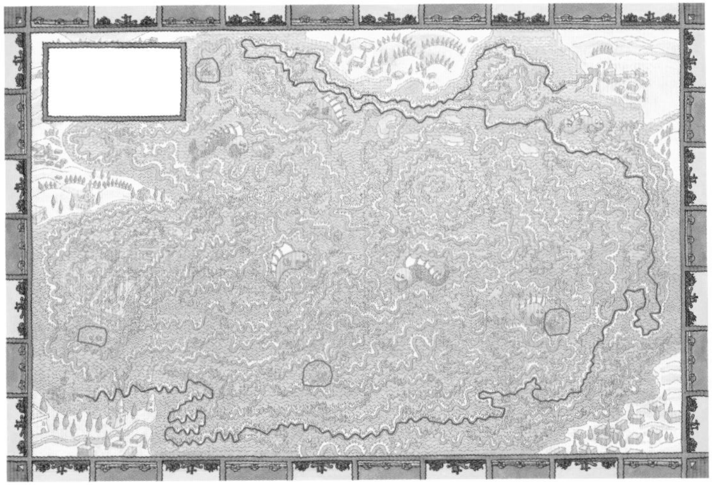

The Mediterranean

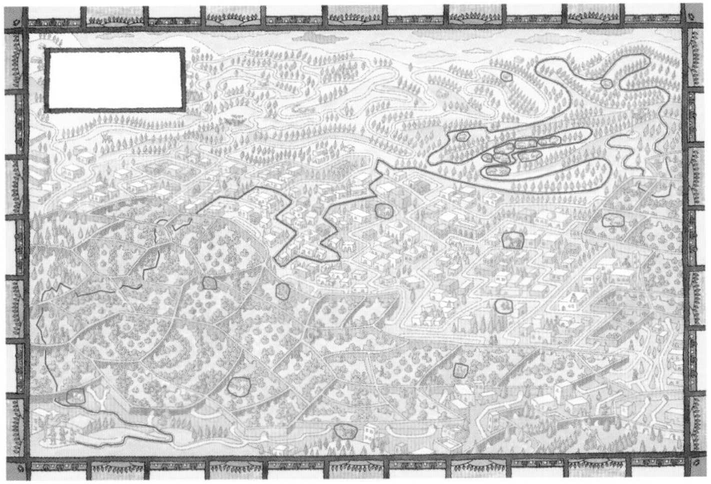

Ezerum

Venice

Jerusalem

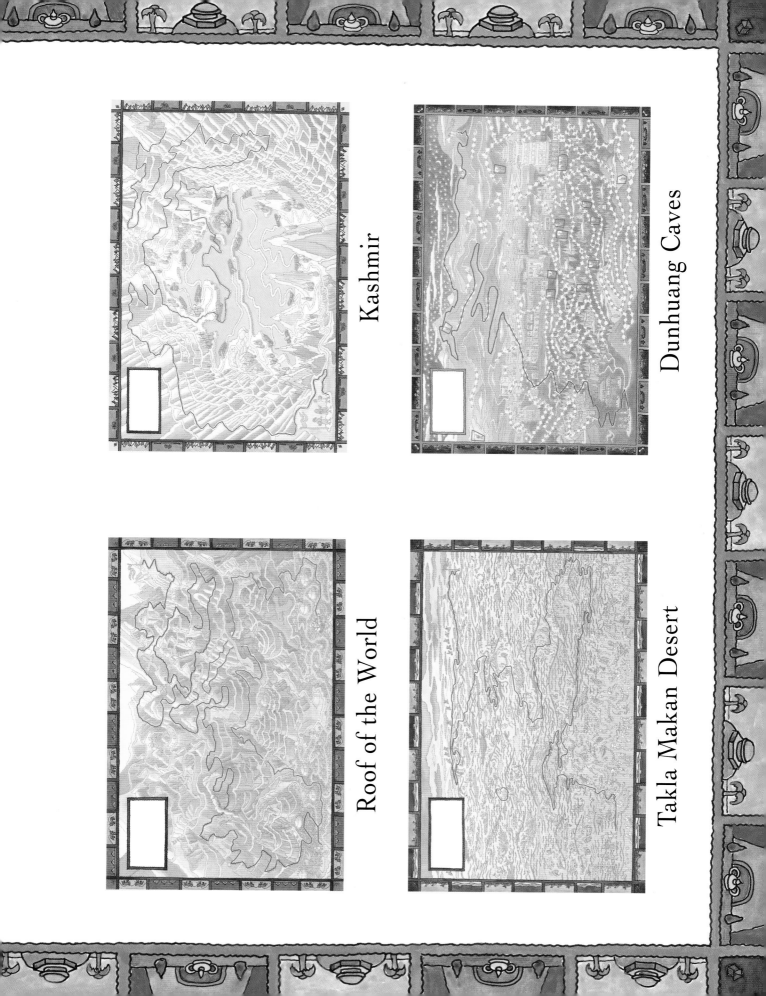

Kashmir

Dunhuang Caves

Roof of the World

Takla Makan Desert

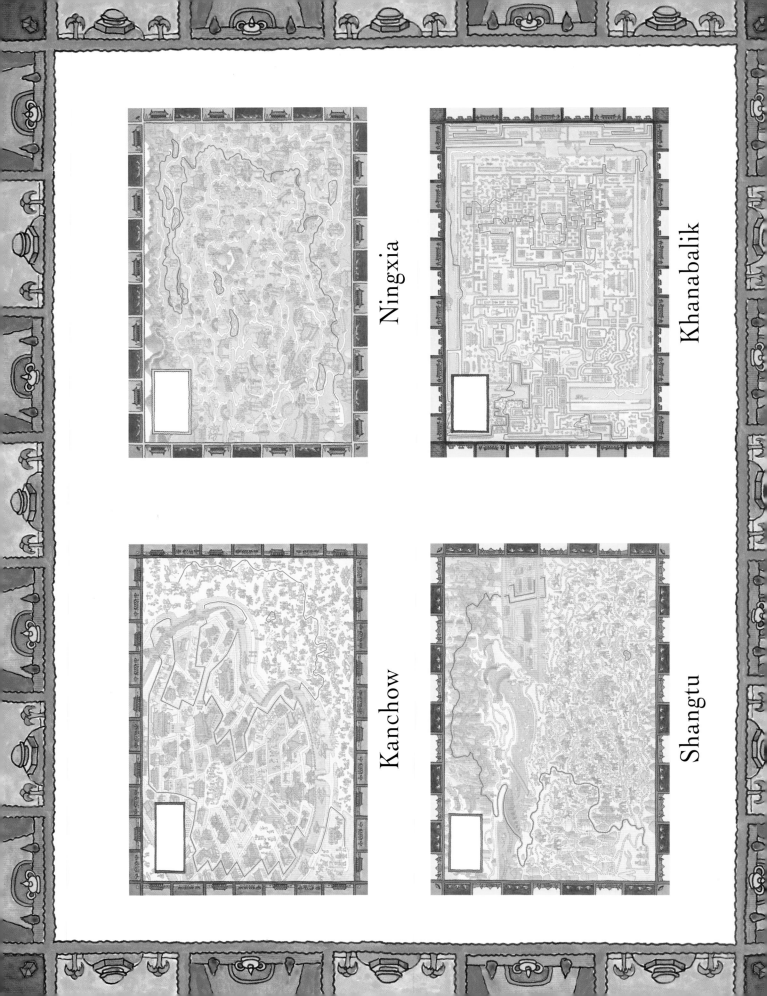

Ningxia

Khanabalik

Kanchow

Shangtu

The aMAZEing voyage of...
CHARLES DARWIN

ANNA NILSEN

For My Digital Hero, Arfan
— from ATB

It's an incredible journey!

Join Charles Darwin on an amazing voyage of discovery. In 1831, he set sail aboard the *Beagle* on a five-year scientific expedition from England to South America. As the ship's naturalist, Darwin studied plant and animal species—and his theories changed scientific thinking forever.

Be prepared for incredible sights! You'll see giant fossils of extinct animals, climb treacherous volcanoes and explore the wonders of the Galapagos Islands.

Start each maze at the green flag and find your way to the red flag. (Can't find the flags? Check their positions in the instructions box for each maze.) After you have returned safely to Plymouth at the end of the book, turn the page and find 12 extra puzzles to challenge your skills of observation.

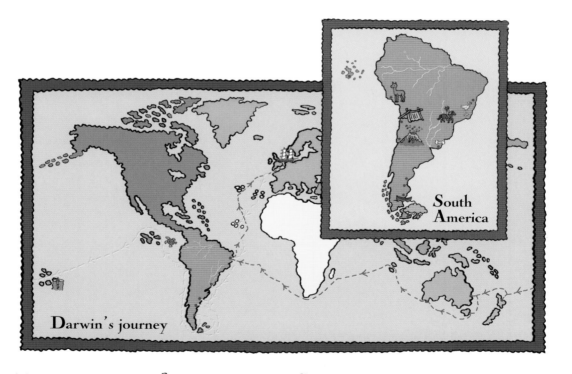

Darwin's journey

South America

Plymouth

Rio Negro

Punta Alta

Tapalguen

Santa Cruz

Tierra del Fuego

Chiloé

Concepción

The Andes

Galapagos Islands

Tahiti

Plymouth

All aboard! Help Darwin find his way to the *Beagle* so the voyage can begin.

Rio Negro

Scramble up the forest vines, then tread gently between the pink flamingos as you wade across the salt lake.

Punta Alta

Find a path from the ship to your tent, stepping carefully through the bone fossils littering the beach.

Tapalguen

Dodge the racing cowboys—and mind you don't get caught in a lasso!

Santa Cruz

Glide along the river's twisting currents
—but don't glide into a tapir!

Tierra del Fuego

Watch out for bolts of lightning as you island hop through stormy seas!

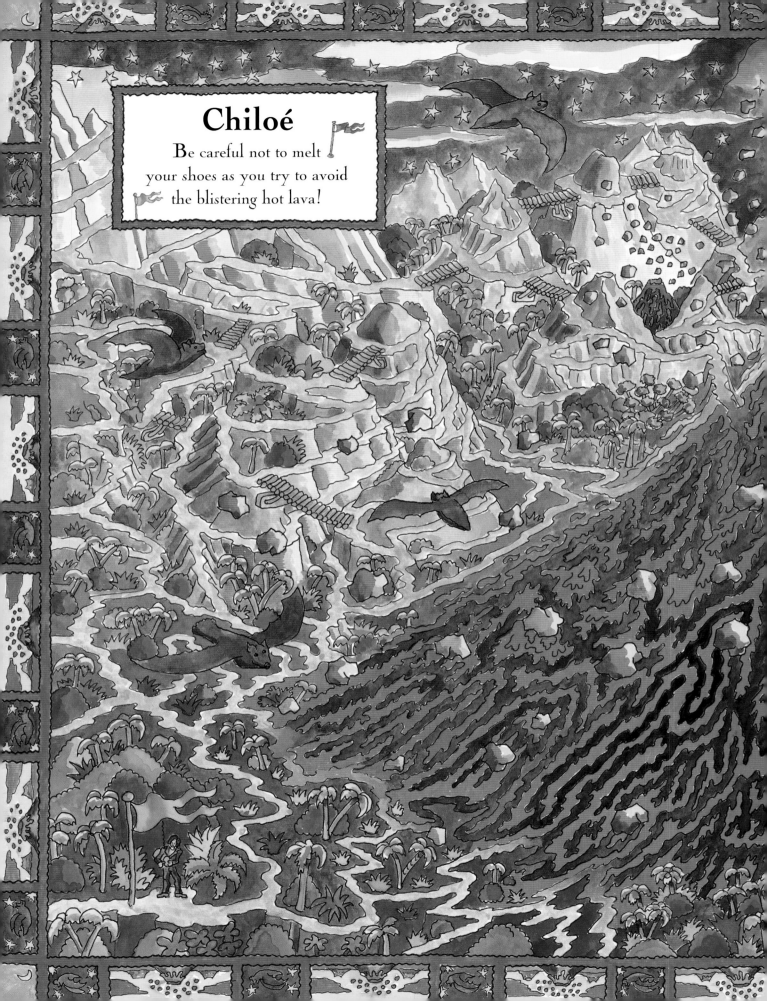

Chiloé

Be careful not to melt your shoes as you try to avoid the blistering hot lava!

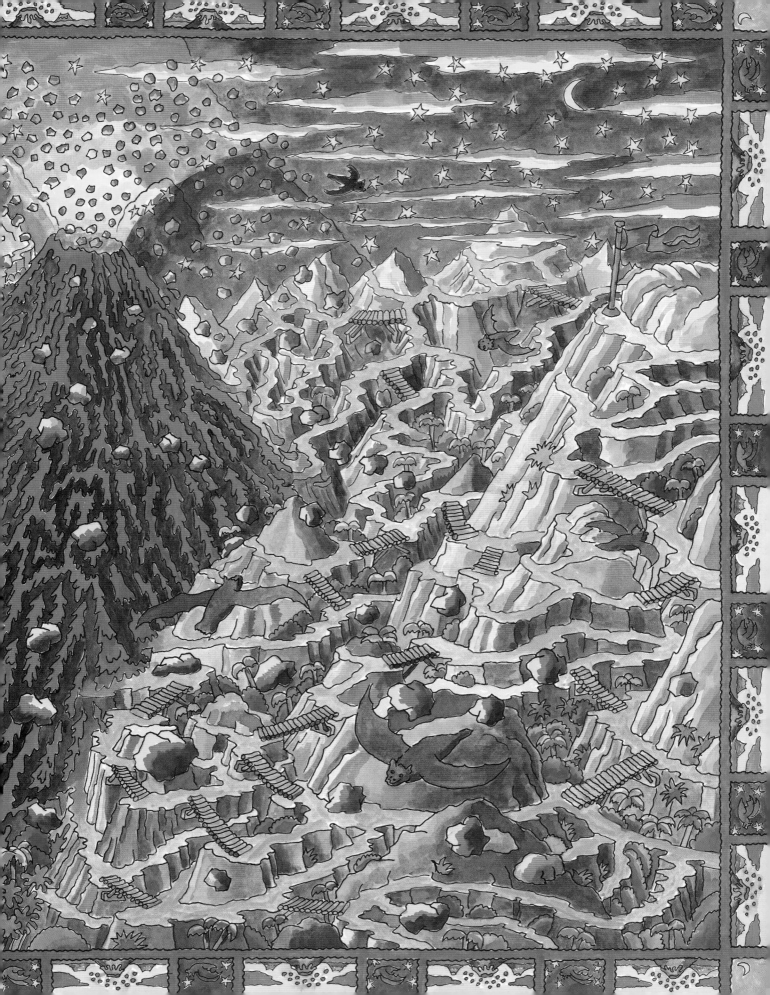

Concepción

Take care not to step on a crack
in this town, which was
devastated by an earthquake.

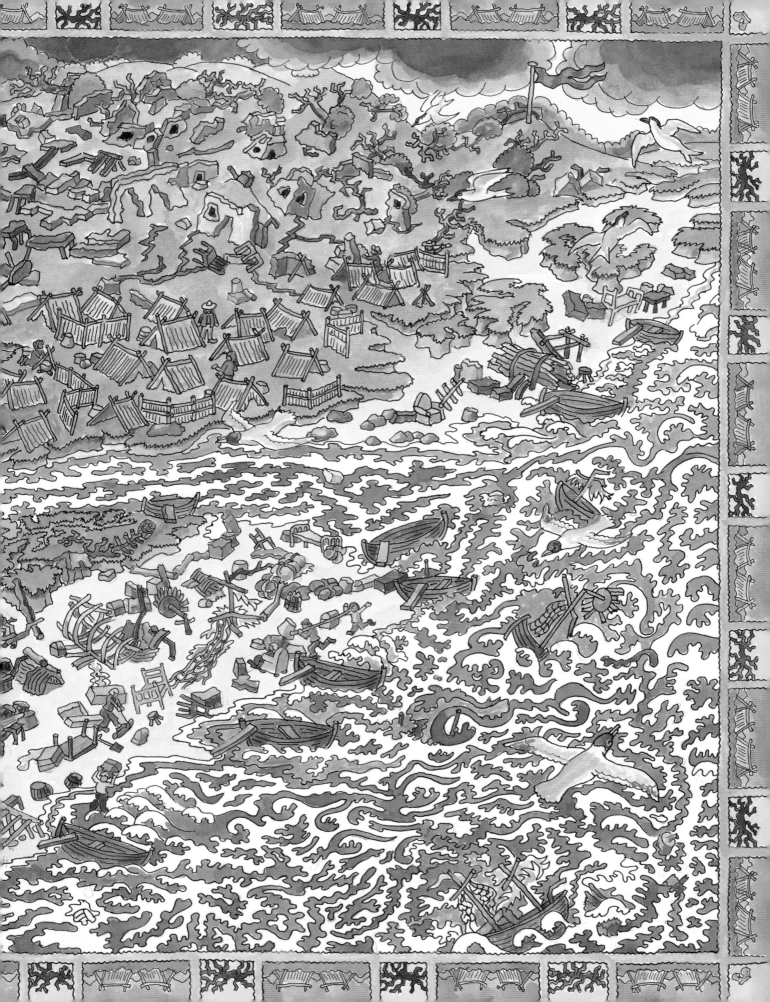

The Andes

Scale the highest peaks of the icy Andes. You can use the guide ropes to help you on the slippery slopes.

Galapagos Islands

Weave between the tortoises and iguanas on land, and use the turtles as stepping-stones across the sea!

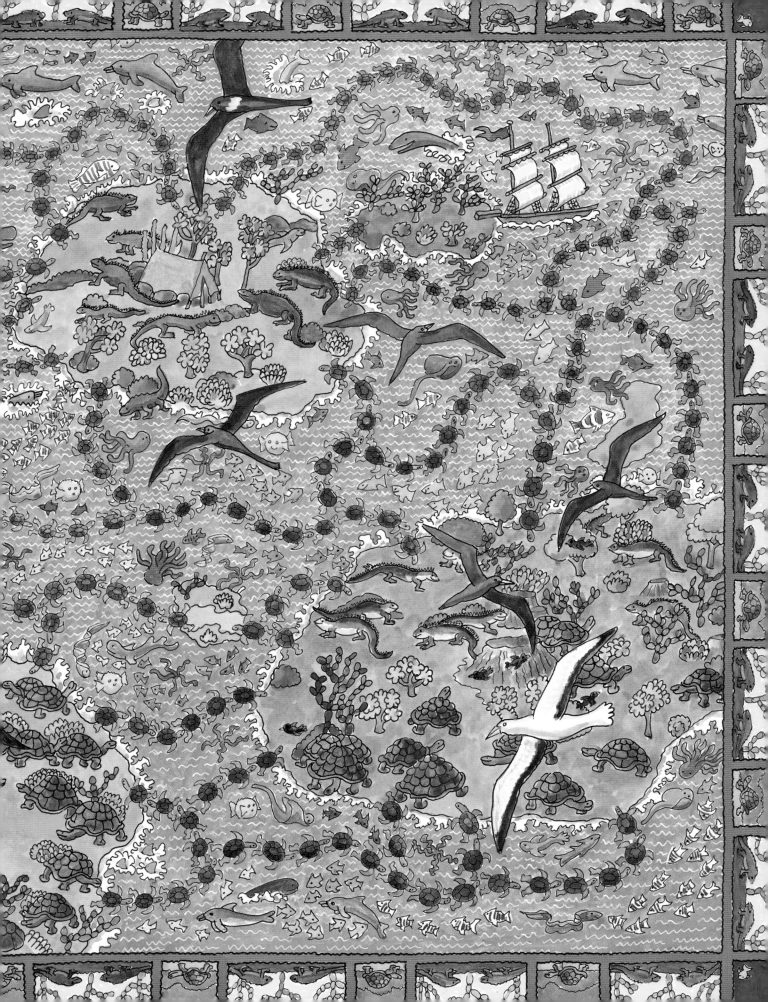

Tahiti

Climb the cliffs of this tropical paradise, using the ropes to clamber from ledge to ledge.

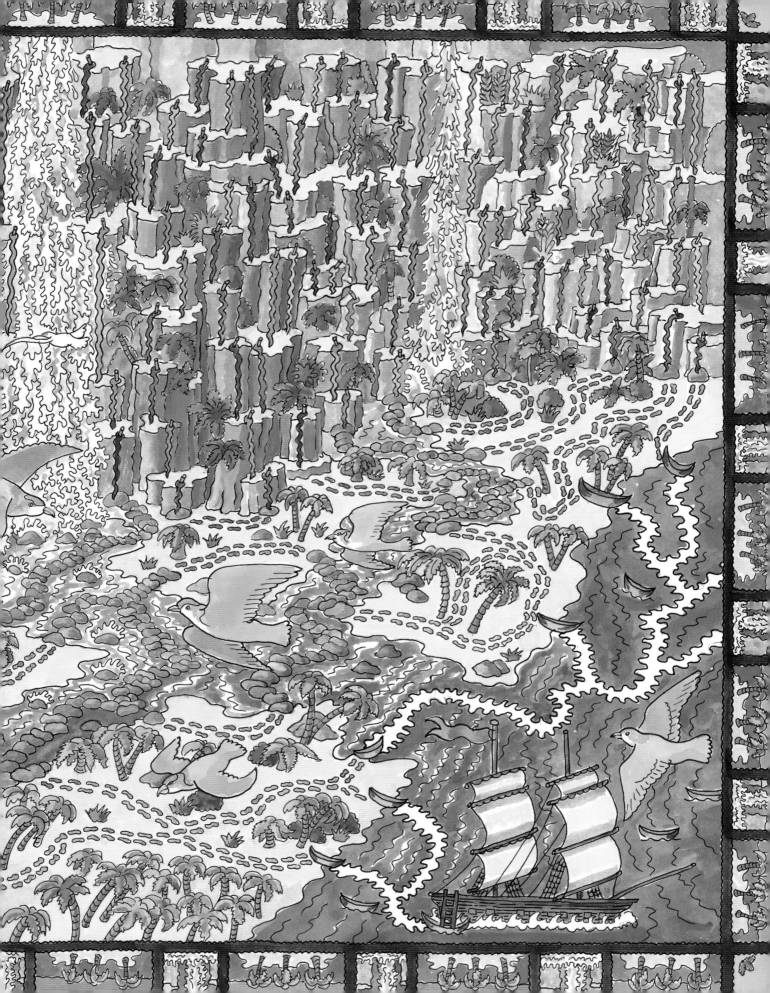

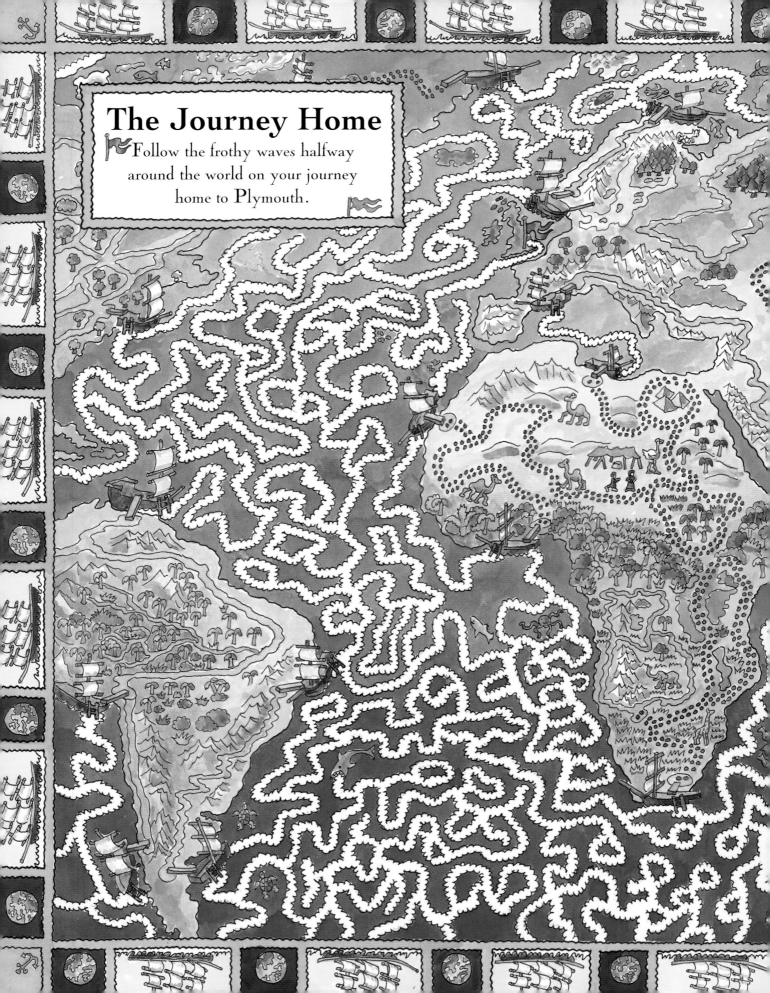

The Journey Home

Follow the frothy waves halfway around the world on your journey home to Plymouth.

Puzzles

Now you be the naturalist! Test your observation skills with the following puzzles.

Plymouth

Can you find a microscope?

Rio Negro

Can you spot a green parrot?

Punta Alta

How many storm petrels can you find?

Tapalguen

Can you find a rhea?

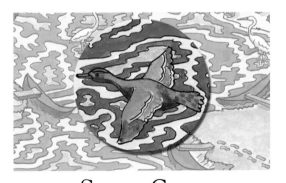

Santa Cruz

How many cinammon teals can you see?

Tierra del Fuego

Can you find seven rufous-legged owls?

Chiloé

How many bats can you see?

Concepción

How many common terns can you spot?

Andes

Can you spot a puma?

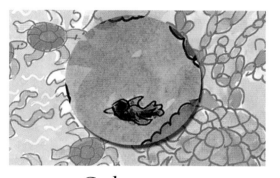

Galapagos

Can you find five Darwin's finches?

Tahiti

How many superb fruit doves can you find?

Journey Home

How many kangaroos can you see?

Solutions!

These are the most direct routes through the mazes.

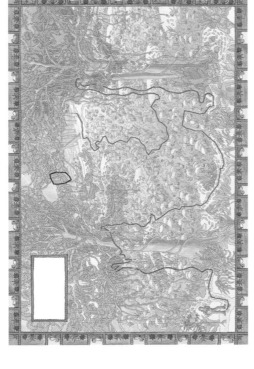

Rio Negro

Tapalguen

Plymouth

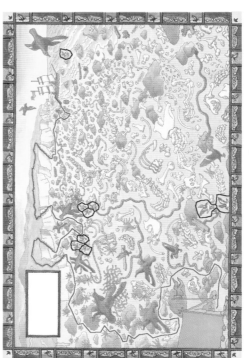

Punta Alta